The Usborne Piano Course

Book One

Katie Elliott and Kathy Gemmell

Original music and arrangements by Katie Elliott

Illustrated by Simone Abel

Designed by Sarah Bealham

Design consultant: Russell Punter

Edited by Emma Danes

Series editor: Anthony Marks

Your piano

How music works

Music is made up of lots of sounds called notes. You play notes by pressing the keys on your piano.

If you look at the black and white keys, you will see that they are arranged in a regular pattern.

Each key on your piano plays a different note. It has a name to go with the note it plays.

ABCDEFGABCDEFG

As you go up the white keys, the note names go from A to G, then start again with A.

Black keys come in groups of two or groups of three.

There are white keys all the way up.

For the tunes in this book, you will only need the white keys.

In this picture, there are letters on the keys to show you which note each one plays.

G A B C D E G

Finding notes

One of the most important notes in this book is called Middle C. The key that plays Middle C is just below the two black keys nearest the middle of the keyboard.

The right-hand end of the piano is called the top because it plays the high notes. The left-hand end is called the bottom because it plays the low notes.

This is Middle C.

Press a key at each end of the piano. Can you hear how different the notes sound?

The bottom of the piano is at the left-hand end.

The top of the piano is at the right-hand end.

Everywhere you find a group of two black keys you will find a C just below it. But there is only one Middle C.

Middle C

A · C D · G A

Can you find and play Middle C on your piano?

Press hard enough to make a clear sound...

...but don't bang!

3

Your first note

On the last page you found out how to play Middle C. Now you can find out how this note is written down in music.

There are two ways to write Middle C. One is for when you play it with your right hand, and one is for when you play it with your left hand.

This is how Middle C is written when you play it with your right hand.

This is how Middle C is written when you play it with your left hand.

Looking at music

Below you can see how notes are written down.

Music is written on a set of five lines called a staff.

The notes fit on the lines...

...and in the spaces.

The notes at the top of the staff sound higher than the notes at the bottom of the staff.

The word for more than one staff is staves. Most piano music is written on two staves, one for each hand.

A curly bracket shows you to play the two staves together. At the beginning of each staff, there is a special sign called a clef.

The treble clef is used for high notes. Play them with your right hand.

Curly bracket

Treble clef

Bass clef

The bass clef is used for low notes. Play them with your left hand.

Middle C in the right hand needs to go below the staff. It has its own short line.

In the left hand, Middle C sits on its own short line just above the staff.

4

Counting

Music is made up of notes of different lengths. You measure the lengths by counting. Each count is called a beat. The pattern of counts in a tune is called its rhythm.

Count evenly up to four a few times.

Don't slow down, or get faster.

Keep counting evenly!

One, two, three, four
One, two, three, four
One, two, three, four
One, two, three, four

Counting and clapping

Try counting evenly to four again, clapping once for each number. Listen to the steady rhythm you are making.

Each clap lasts for one even count or beat. When you see a note written down, its shape tells you how long it lasts.

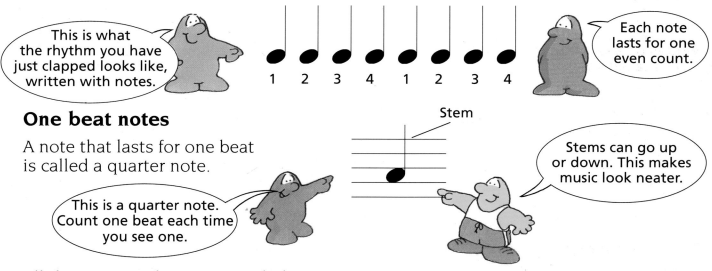

This is what the rhythm you have just clapped looks like, written with notes.

1 2 3 4 1 2 3 4

Each note lasts for one even count.

One beat notes

A note that lasts for one beat is called a quarter note.

Stem

Stems can go up or down. This makes music look neater.

This is a quarter note. Count one beat each time you see one.

All the notes in the two tunes below are quarter notes.

C tune

C tune too

Look at the clefs to see which hand to use.

Make sure you count and play evenly.

Press the key down with your thumb. Lift it and do exactly the same for the next note in the tune.

What music looks like

When music is written down, it is usually split into sections called bars.

Bars make it easier to see where you are in the music and how many beats you have already counted.

How long is a bar?

The numbers written beside the clef tell you how many beats there are in each bar.

These two numbers together are called the time signature.

Longer notes

All the notes you have played so far have been quarter notes, which last for one beat. A note that lasts for two counts, or beats, is called a half note.

A note that lasts for four beats is called a whole note.

This is a half note. Count two beats when you see a half note.

This is a whole note. Count four beats when you see a whole note.

More note clapping

Try to clap the rhythm below. First count from one to four a few times, making sure you count evenly.

Then fit the claps to the counts, clapping each time you see this sign: *. You should clap once for each note.

There are four beats in each bar.

The numbers show you how to count.

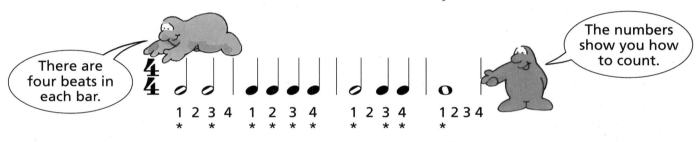

```
1 2 3 4   1 2 3 4   1 2 3 4   1 2 3 4
*   *     * * * *   *  * *    *
```

C *for two*

Here is a tune for you to play using all the notes you have learned so far.

Clap the rhythm first, counting out loud, then fit the notes into the rhythm.

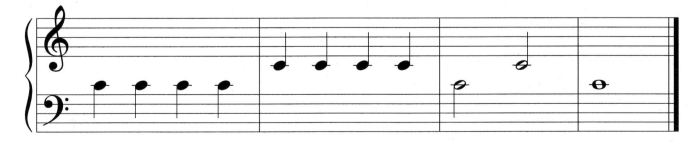

7

A new note

In the tune below there is a new note for the right hand, called D. On the right you can see what D looks like on the staff, and where to find it on the piano.

D in the treble clef sits just below the bottom line.

D is always between the black notes in a group of two. Find and play every D on your piano.

Middle C   D

Fingers and numbers

Sometimes in music you will see a number above a note. This tells you which finger you should use to play it.

Below you can see which number goes with each finger. Hold up your hands and say the number of each of your fingers.

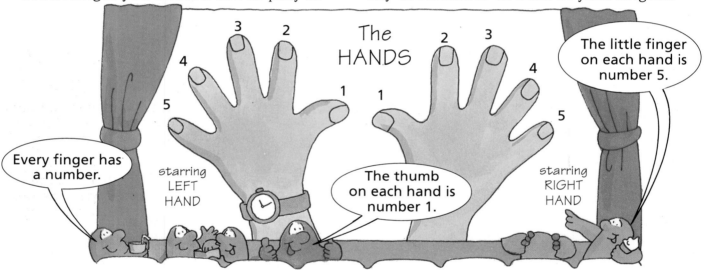

The HANDS

starring LEFT HAND

starring RIGHT HAND

Every finger has a number.

The thumb on each hand is number 1.

The little finger on each hand is number 5.

Traffic jam

For all the tunes in this book, you keep your hands in the same position. Make sure you use the correct finger for each note, every time.

Both your thumbs stay over Middle C.

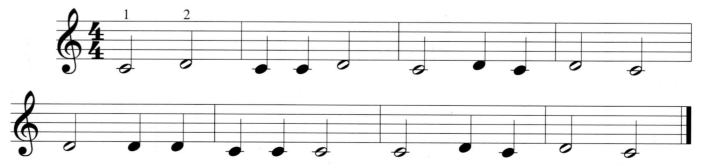

More rhythm clapping

Have a good look at this rhythm, then see if you can clap it.

Remember, bar lines are there to make it easier to see where you are in the music...

...so you don't need to stop at each one.

Note lengths

This picture will help you remember how long whole notes, half notes and quarter notes last.

whole note = 4

half note 2 + 2 = 4

quarter note 1 + 1 + 1 + 1 = 4

A half note lasts for the same number of beats as two quarter notes.

One whole note lasts for the same number of beats as two half notes or four quarter notes.

Muddy march

Here is a tune to play with both hands. Try playing Middle C a few times with each thumb in turn before you start.

Don't worry if it looks difficult at first.

Clap through the rhythm before you start playing.

Are you sitting comfortably?

The next tune has a new note for the left hand, called B. On the right, you can see what it looks like on the staff and where to find it on your piano.

In the bass clef, B sits just above the top line.

B is the white key to the right of a group of three black keys. See if you can find every B on your piano.

B Middle C

Creepy-crawlies

Here is a tune to play with your left hand on its own.

Play B with the second finger of your left hand a few times before you begin.

Look out for the numbers which tell you which fingers to use.

How to sit

When you play the piano sit up straight, but make sure you don't feel uncomfortable. This will help you play without getting tired.

Find Middle C and sit in front of it.

Rest your hands lightly on the keys with your fingers curved down slightly.

Sign search

There are seven musical signs or notes hidden in this picture. Can you find and name them all?

Look back at the first ten pages of this book if you can't remember all the names.

Hold your wrists so the backs of your hands and arms are level.

Take care not to hunch your shoulders.

You shouldn't have to reach up or down to the keys. Make sure your chair isn't too high.

If it is too low, sit on a cushion.

11

Tunes for two people

Some music is for two people to play together. When you can play the tune on page 13 without any mistakes, ask a good piano player to join in by playing the tune on this page at the same time.

Tunes for two people are called duets.

Elephant dance (accompaniment)

This tune fits together with the tune on the opposite page. It is called an accompaniment.

Don't worry! This is for your someone who is good at the piano (like your teacher) to play.

Which of you sounds like the biggest elephant?

Repeats

At the end of the tune below, you will find a special sign called a repeat.

Elephant dance

Still sitting comfortably?

In the next tune your right hand plays another new note, called E. Look at E on the staff, and at where to find it on the piano.

E in the treble clef is on the bottom line.

Middle C   E

E is the white key to the right of a group of two black keys. Can you find every E on your piano?

Merrily we roll along

Before you start to play this tune, play E a few times with the third finger of your right hand.

Try clapping the rhythm and counting the beats first. Then work out what the notes are.

Sitting up straight

Remember how important it is to sit properly, with your back straight, right in front of Middle C.

Be very careful not to flatten your fingers over the keys.

Keep your fingers curved down from your hand and press the keys with your fingertips.

It is much harder to play with your fingers sticking out straight.

New note search

On the right you can see all the notes you have learned so far. See how quickly you can find each note on your piano and play it (with the correct hand, of course).

A new time signature

The tune on this page has a different time signature from the tunes you have played so far. It has a three on top.

The three on top means there are three beats to count in every bar.

Remember, the four on the bottom tells you that each beat is a quarter note.

Always look for the time signature at the beginning of a tune.

Folk song

This is a German tune. First clap the rhythm and then work out the notes.

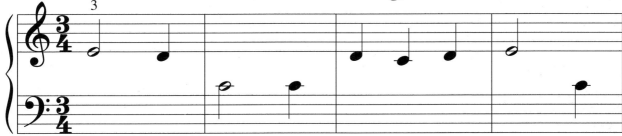

Remember, there are only three beats to count in each bar.

Another new note

The new note in the next tune is an A for your left hand. On the right, you can see what it looks like on the staff and where to find it on your piano.

A in the bass clef is on the top line of the staff.

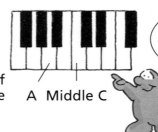

A   Middle C

Find a group of three black keys. A is the white key between the top two black keys.

Totem poles

Here is a tune for both hands to play. Practice playing A a few times with the third finger of your left hand before you start.

Three-beat notes

A half note with a dot after it is called a dotted half note. It lasts for three beats instead of two.

A dot after a note makes the note last for half as long again.

Clap the rhythm

Lady Elizabeth's air

Playing quietly

There are special words in music that tell you how loudly or quietly to play.

The word that tells you to play quietly is *piano*. This is Italian for "quiet".

Piano is usually shortened to *p*.

Crossing the River Volga

To play quietly, press the key gently. But make sure the notes sound properly.

Don't slow down when you play quietly.

You will find *p* between the staves, like this:

Playing loudly

The word that tells you to play loudly is *forte*. This is Italian for "loud".

Forte is usually shortened to *f*.

To play a note *forte* press the key hard, but don't bang it.

Barn dance

Make sure both your thumbs are over Middle C.

Remember to play loudly when you see *f*...

...and quietly when you see *p*.

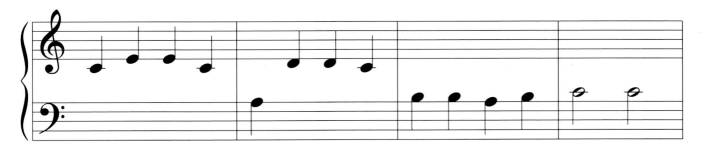

Playing G

The next tune has a new note in the left hand, called G. On the right you can see G on a staff, and where to find it on a piano.

G sits on the space below the top line.

Find a group of three black keys. G is the white key between the bottom two.

G   Middle C

Au clair de la lune

This tune was written in the 17th century by a French composer called Lully.

Play G a few times with the fourth finger of your left hand before you start.

See if you can find every G on your piano.

Sight-reading

Playing a new piece for the first time is called sight-reading. There are many ways to make sight-reading easier.

With a bit of detective work, you can find lots of clues about a piece before you start to play.

Before you play

1. The top number of the time signature tells you how many beats to count in each bar. The bottom number, 4, tells you that each beat is a quarter note.

sssshhhhhh !

2. Look for words or signs which tell you how loudly or quietly to play.

3. Clap the rhythms before you start to play. Find any new notes and practice them a few times. Don't start playing too fast.

Starting to play

When you first play a piece, try to keep going to the end, even if you play a wrong note. Then go back to practice any difficult parts.

Don't start again if you go wrong...

...otherwise you only practice the part you can already play.

Air des bouffons

This tune was played in France hundreds of years ago. People danced to it with swords. The dance was called *bouffons*.

Remember to look for clues in the music before you start to play.

Which finger?

Here is a new right-hand note, called F. On the right, you can see what F looks like on a staff and where to find it on the piano.

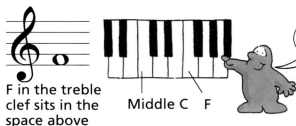

F in the treble clef sits in the space above the bottom line.

Middle C   F

F is the white key to the left of a group of three black keys.

The F finger

In the next few tunes, you are going to play F with the fourth finger of your right hand.

Play this a few times to help make your fourth finger stronger.

Press evenly on each key.

Giants

This tune comes from Sweden. Think of big, heavy giants when you play the parts that have *forte* signs below them. Make these notes sound big and strong.

Remember not to bang the keys!

Use your right hand!

Another rhythm

Here is a rhythm for you to clap. Look at it carefully before you start.

Can you remember how many beats each note lasts for?

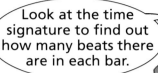

Look at the time signature to find out how many beats there are in each bar.

Soeur Monique

This tune was written by a French composer called Couperin. Its title means "Sister Monica".

Remember to look at all the notes before you start to play.

An old tune: *Yankee Doodle*

You may already know this tune.

Yankee Doodle quiz

Here are some questions about Yankee Doodle. Play the tune again to help you. You can find the answers on page 27.

Note spotting

You have already played G with your left hand, so here's a G for your right hand. Look at what a right-hand G looks like on the staff and where to find it on your piano.

G in the treble clef sits on the second line up.

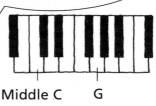

Remember, G is the white key between the bottom two black keys of a group of three.

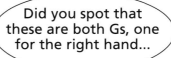

Middle C   G

Play the left hand G and then the right hand G. Which one sounds higher?

Note check

Here are some notes in both the treble and bass clefs. Can you name them all and find them on your piano?

Did you spot that these are both Gs, one for the right hand...

...and one for the left hand?

Little John

Play the first G of this tune with the little finger of your right hand.

You will then have enough fingers to play all the other notes.

More sight-reading

Before you try the tune below, look for clues about how to play it.

What do all the signs mean?

How many beats are there in each bar?

Which bars should be loud and which ones quiet?

Which hand do you start with?

Good King Wenceslas

Note quiz

Can you answer these note questions? The answers are at the bottom of the page.

Each time you answer a question, see if you can play that note on your piano.

Which note is the ballerina standing on?

What is this note called?

What is this note called?

Who is playing this note?

This is the middle section of a piano.

Who is standing on Middle C?

Who is playing an F?

Answers

Page 24

There are four beats in each bar. The highest note is an F. The sign _p_ tells you to play quietly.

Page 27

The ballerina is standing on G in the bass clef. The first treble clef note is D. The cowgirl is playing A in the bass clef. The second treble clef note is G. The surfer is standing on Middle C. The bride is playing an F.

Using your little finger

The next tune uses another new note for the left hand. This time it is an F. You can see on the right what it looks like on the staff and where to find it on your piano.

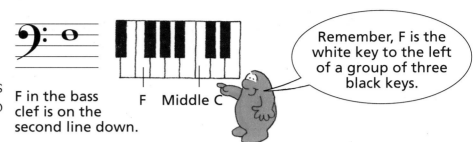

F in the bass clef is on the second line down.

F   Middle C

Remember, F is the white key to the left of a group of three black keys.

Getting fit with F

Sometimes, you have to play F with the little finger of your left hand.

Often, this finger isn't as strong as your other ones. Play the notes below to help it.

Play the notes evenly, counting 1 for each quarter note...

...and 2 for each half note.

Banana skins

If you find playing the F in this tune a bit difficult, play the notes above again. Or play F a few times with your little finger before you begin.

Both hands together

In the tune below, you play with both hands at the same time. When you try it for the first time, don't play it too quickly.

Make sure you hold the left hand notes for the full four beats while the right hand continues playing.

Peculiar polka

Are there any parts you find more difficult than the rest? Practice these separately a few times before you play the whole tune again.

Practicing will stop you from slowing down when you get to the difficult bars...

...or from making the same mistake over and over again!

Playing duts

You can play *Heaps of Hippopotami* on your own or as a duet. Your part is on page 31. If you want to play it as a duet, play your part higher up the piano than usual.

This way, both of you can sit comfortably. Instead of starting your part on Middle C, put your thumb on the next C up. Pretend this C is Middle C when you play.

Heaps of Hippopotami (accompaniment)

The music below is for someone who is good at the piano to play.

Ask him or her to play it at the same time as you play the tune opposite.

New music signs

There is a new kind of repeat in the tune below.

D.C. is short for the Italian *da capo* which means "from the top".

When you reach *D.C. al fine*, go back to the beginning of the tune. Play it again until you come to the word *Fine*.

Fine means "the end" in Italian...

...so you stop.

Heaps of Hippopotami

Make sure you can play this tune well on your own before you try to play it with someone else.

If you want to play this as a duet, look first at the page opposite.

Your last tune: *Party Piece*

Most of the time in this tune, your hands will be doing exactly the same thing.

First published in 1994 by Usborne Publishing Ltd., Usborne House, 83-85 Saffron Hill, London EC1N 8RT, England.
Copyright © 2008, 1994 Usborne Publishing Ltd. Printed in Portugal. First Published in America, March 1995. AE